# THE SPIRITUAL COUPLETS
## OF
## MAULANA JALALU-'D-DIN
## MUHAMMAD RUMI

*Abridged and Translated*

*E.H. Whinfield*

## Masnavi
## Book 5

[ZHINGOORA BOOKS]

STORY I.

The Prophet and his Infidel Guest.
AFTER the usual address to Husamu-'d-Din follows a comment on
the precept addressed to Abraham, "Take four birds and draw them
towards thee, and cut them in pieces."1 The birds are explained to
be the duck of gluttony, the cock of concupiscence, the peacock of
ambition and ostentation, and the crow of bad desires, and this is
made the text of several stories. Beginning with gluttony, the poet
tells the following story to illustrate the occasion of the Prophet's
uttering the saying, Infidels eat with seven bellies, but the faithful
with one." One day some infidels begged food and lodging of the
Prophet. The Prophet was moved by their entreaties, and desired
each of his disciples to take one of the infidels to his house and feed
and lodge him, remarking that it was their duty to show kindness to
strangers at his command, as much as to do battle with his foes. So
each disciple selected one of the infidels and carried him off to his
house; but there was one big and coarse man, a very giant Og,
whom no one would receive, and the Prophet took him to his own
house. In his house the Prophet had seven she-goats to supply his
family with milk, and the hungry infidel devoured all the milk of
those seven goats, to say nothing of bread and other viands. He left
not a drop for the Prophet's family, who were therefore much
annoyed with him, and when he retired to his chamber one of the
servant-maids locked him in. During the night the infidel felt very
unwell in consequence of having overeaten himself, and tried to get
out into the open air, but was unable to do so, owing to the door
being locked. Finally, he was very sick, and defiled his bedding. In
the morning he was extremely ashamed, and the moment the door
was opened he ran away. The Prophet was aware of what had
happened, but let the man escape, so as not to put him to shame.
After he had gone the servants saw the mess he had made, and

2

informed the Prophet of it; but the Prophet made light of it, and said he would clean it up himself. His friends were shocked at the thought of the Prophet soiling his sacred hands with such filth, and tried to prevent him, but he persisted in doing it, calling to mind the text, "As thou livest, O Muhammad, they were bewildered by drunkenness," 2 and being, in fact, urged to it by a divine command. While he was engaged in the work the infidel came back to look for a talisman which he had left behind him in his hurry to escape, and seeing the Prophet's occupation he burst into tears, and bewailed his own filthy conduct. The Prophet consoled him, saying that weeping and penitence would purge the offence, for God says, "Little let them laugh, and much let them weep;" 3 and again, "Lend God a liberal loan;" 4 and again, "God only desireth to put away filthiness from you as His household, and with cleansing to cleanse you." 5 Prophet then urged him to bear witness that God was the Lord, even as was done by the sons of Adam, 6 explained how the outward acts of prayer and fasting bear witness of the spiritual light within. After being nurtured on this spiritual food the infidel confessed the truth of Islam, and renounced his infidelity and gluttony. He returned thanks to the Prophet for bringing him to the knowledge of the true faith and regenerating him, even as 'Isa had regenerated Lazarus. The Prophet was satisfied of his sincerity, and asked him to sup with him again. At supper he drank only half the portion of milk yielded by one goat, and steadfastly refused to take more, saying he felt perfectly satisfied with the little he had already taken. The other guests marveled much to see his gluttony so soon cured, and were led to reflect on the virtues of the spiritual food administered to him by the Prophet.

Outward acts bear witness of the state of the heart within.
Prayer and fasting and pilgrimage and holy war
Bear witness of the faith of the heart.
Giving alms and offerings and quitting avarice
Also bear witness of the secret thoughts.
So, a table spread for guests serves as a plain sign,
Saying, "O guest, I am your sincere well-wisher."
So, offerings and presents and oblations

Bear witness, saying, "I am well pleased with you."
Each of these men lavishes his wealth or pains,
What means it but to say, "I have a virtue within me,
Yea, a virtue of piety or liberality,
Whereof my oblations and fasting bear witness"?
Fasting proclaims that he abstains from lawful food,
And that therefore he doubtless avoids unlawful food.
And his alms say, "He gives away his own goods;
It is therefore plain that he does not rob others."
If he acts thus from fraud, his two witnesses
(Fasting and alms) are rejected in God's court;
If the hunter scatters grain
Not out of mercy, but to catch game;
If the cat keeps fast, and remains still
In fasting only to entrap unwary birds;
Making hundreds of people suspicious,
And giving a bad name to men who fast and are liberal;
Yet the grace of God, despite this fraud,
May ultimately purge him from all this hypocrisy.
Mercy may prevail over vengeance, and give the hypocrite
Such light as is not possessed by the full moon.
God may purge his dealings from that hypocrisy,
And in mercy wash him clean of that defilement.
In order that the pardoning grace of God may be seen,
God pardons all sins that need pardon.
Wherefore God rains down water from the sign Pisces,
To purify the impure from their impurities. 7
Thus acts and words are witnesses of the mind within,
From these two deduce inferences as to the thoughts.
When your vision cannot penetrate within,
Inspect the water voided by the sick man.
Acts and words resemble the sick man's water,
Which serves as evidence to the physician of the body.
But the physician of the spirit penetrates the soul,
And thence ascertains the man's faith.
Such an one needs not the evidence of fair acts and words

4

"Beware of such, they spy out the heart."
Require this evidence of act and word only from one
Who is not joined to the divine Ocean like a stream.
But the light of the traveler arrived at the goal,
Verily that light fills deserts and wastes.
That witness of his is exempt from bearing witness,
And from all trouble and risk and good works.
Since the brilliance of that jewel beams forth,
It is exempted from these obligations.
Wherefore require not from him act and word evidence,
Because both worlds through him bloom like roses.
What is this evidence but manifestation of hidden things,
Whether it be evidence in word, or deed, or otherwise?
Accidents serve only to manifest the secret essence;
The essential quality abides, and accidents pass away.
This mark of gold endures not the touchstone,
But only the gold itself, genuine and undoubted.
These prayers and holy war and fasting
Will not endure, only the noble soul endures.
The soul exhibits acts and words of this sort,
Then it rubs its substance on the touchstone of God's command,
Saying, "My faith is true, behold my witnesses!"
But witnesses are open to suspicion.
Know that witnesses must be purified,
And their purification is sincerity, on that you may depend.
The witness of word consists in speaking the truth,
The witness of acts in keeping one's promises.
If the witness of word lie, its evidence is rejected,
And if the witness of act play false, it is rejected.
Your words and acts must be without self-contradiction
In order to be accepted without question.
"Your aims are different," 8 and you contradict yourselves,
You sew by day, and tear to pieces by night.
How can God listen to such contradictory witness,
Unless He be pleased to decide on it in mercy?
Act and word manifest the secret thoughts and mind,

5

Both of them expose to view the veiled secret.
When your witnesses are purified they are accepted,
Otherwise they are arrested and kept in durance.
They enter into conflict with you, O stiff-necked one;
"Stand aloof and wait for them, for they too wait." 9
Prayers for spiritual enlightenment.
O God, who hast no peer, bestow Thy favor upon me;
Since Thou hast with this discourse put a ring in my ear,
Take me by the ear, and draw me into that holy assembly
Where Thy saints in ecstasy drink of Thy pure wine!
Now that Thou hast caused me to smell its perfume,
Withhold not from me that musky wine, O Lord of faith
Of Thy bounty all partake, both men and women,
Thou art ungrudging in bounties, O Hearer of prayer.
Prayers are granted by Thee before they are uttered,
Thou openest the door to admit hearts every moment!
How many letters Thou writest with Thy Almighty pen!
Through marveling thereat stones become as wax.
Thou writest the Nun of the brow, the Sad of the eye,
And the Jim of the ear, to amaze reason and sense.
These letters exercise and perplex reason;
Write on, O skilful Fair-writer!
Imprinting every moment on Not-being the fair forms
Of the world of ideals, to confound all thought! 10
Yea, copying thereon the fair letters of the page of ideals,
To wit, eye and brow and moustache and mole!
For me, I will be a lover of Not-being, not of existence,
Because the beloved of Not-being is more blessed. 11
God made reason a reader of all these letters,
To suggest to it reflections on that outpouring of grace. 12
Reason, like Gabriel, learns day by day
Its daily portion from the "Indelible Tablet." 13
Behold the letters written without hands on Not-being!
Behold the perplexity of mankind at those letters!
Every one is bewildered by these thoughts,
And digs for hidden treasure in hope to find it.

This bewilderment of mankind as to their true aims is compared to the bewilderment of men in the dark looking in all directions for the Qibla, and recalls the text, "O the misery that rests upon my servants." 14

Then follow reflections on the sacrifice by Abraham of the peacock of ambition and ostentation. Next comes a discourse on the thesis that all men can recognize the mercies of God and the wrath of God; but God's mercies are often hidden in His chastisements, and vice versa, and it is only men of deep spiritual discernment who can recognize acts of mercy and acts of wrath concealed in their opposites. The object of this concealment is to try and test men's dispositions; according to the text, "To prove which of you will be most righteous in deed." 15

*NOTES:

1. Koran ii. 262.
2. Koran xv. 72.
3. Koran ix. 33.
4. Koran lxxiii. 20.
5. Koran xxxiii. 33.
6. Koran vii. 171.
7. "Islam is the baptism of God" (Koran ii. 132).
8. Koran xcii. 4.
9. Koran xxxii. 30. i.e., Wait thou for their punishment, as they wait for thy downfall (Rodwell).
10. Here we have another Platonic doctrine. "Some say the belief of the Sufis is the same as that of the Ishraqin (Platonists)." Dabistan i Muzahib, by Shea and Troyer, iii. 281.
11. I.e., I will recognize the nonentity of all this phenomenal being, and court self-annihilation.
12. The Bulaq translator renders An naward thus.
13. The "Indelible Tablet" (of God's decrees) is here applied to the Logos-the channel through whom God renews the "world of creation" day by day.
14. Koran xxxvi. 29.
15. Koran lxvii. 2.

STORY II.

The Arab and his Dog.

The doctrine of the Mu'tazilites, 1 mentioned, that all men's intellects are alike and equal at birth, is again controverted, and the poet dwells on the essential differences which characterize the intellects akin to Universal Reason or the Logos, and those swayed by partial or carnal reason; the former, like the children of Israel, seeking exaltation through self-abasement; and the others, like Pharaoh, running after worldly rank and power, to their own destruction. In order to make probation of men, as already explained, God fills the world with deceptions, 2 making apparent blessings destructive to us, and apparent evils salutary. On the other hand, if men try to deceive God, they fail signally. Hypocritical weeping and wailing like that of Joseph's brethren is at once detected by God. Thus a certain Arab had a dog to which he was much attached; but one day the dog died of hunger. He at once began to weep and wail, and disturbed the whole neighborhood by his ostentatious grief One of the neighbors came and inquired into the matter, and on hearing that the dog had died of hunger, he asked the Arab why he had not fed him from the wallet of food which he had in his hand. The Arab said that he had collected this food to support himself, and made it a principle not to part with any of it to any one who could not pay for it; but that, as his tears cost him nothing, he was pouring them forth in token of the sorrow he felt for his dog's death. The neighbor, on hearing this, rebuked him for his hypocrisy, and went his way. Then follows a commentary on the text, "Almost would the infidels strike thee down with their very looks when they hear the reading of the Koran." 3

*NOTES:

1. The Mu'tazilites were one of the principal unorthodox sects. See Sale, Prelim. Disc., p. 112.
2. "Of them who devise stratagems, God is beast" (Koran iii. 47).
3. Koran lxviii. 51.

STORY III.

The Sage and the Peacock.

A sage went out to till his field, and saw a peacock busily engaged in destroying his own plumage with his beak. At seeing this insane self-destruction the sage could not refrain himself, but cried out to the peacock to forbear from mutilating himself and spoiling his beauty in so wanton a manner. The peacock then explained to him that the bright plumage which he admired so much was a fruitful source of danger to its unfortunate owner, as it led to his being constantly pursued by hunters, whom he had no strength to contend against; and he had accordingly decided on ridding himself of it with his own beak, and making himself so ugly that no hunter would in future care to molest him. The poet proceeds to point out that worldly cleverness and accomplishments and wealth endanger man's spiritual life, like the peacock's plumage; but, nevertheless, they are appointed for our probation, and without such trials there can be no virtue.

"There is no monkery in Islam."1

Tear not thy plumage off it cannot be replaced;
Disfigure not thy face in wantonness, O fair one!
That face which is bright as the forenoon sun,
To disfigure it were a grievous sin.
'Twere paganism to mar such a face as thine!
The moon itself would weep to lose sight of it!
Knowest thou not the beauty of thine own face?
Quit this temper that leads thee to war with thyself!
It is the claws of thine own foolish thoughts
That in spite wound the face of thy quiet soul.
Know such thoughts to be claws fraught with poison,
Which score deep wounds on the face of thy soul.
Rend not thy plumage off, but avert thy heart from it
For hostility between them is the law of this holy war.
Were there no hostility, that war would be impossible.
Iladst thou no lust, obedience to the law could not be. 2
Hadst thou no concupiscence there could be no abstinence.

9

Where no antagonist, what need is there of armies?
Ah! make not thyself an eunuch, 3 not a monk,
Because chastity is mortgaged to lust.
Without lust denial of lust is impossible
No man can display bravery against the dead.
God says, "Expend;" 4 wherefore earn money.
Since expenditure is impossible without previous gain?
Although the passage contains only the word "Expend,"
Read "Acquire first, and then expend."
In like manner, when the King of kings says "Abstain," 5
It implies an object of desire wherefrom to abstain.
Again, "Eat ye," is said recognising the snares of lust,
And afterwards, " Exceed not," 6 to enjoin temperance.
When there is no subject,
The existence of a predicate is not possible. 7
When thou endurest not the pains of abstinence
And fulfillest not the terms, thou gainest no reward.
How easy those terms! how abundant that reward!
A reward that enchants the heart and charms the soul!
This is followed by the admonition that the only way to be safe
from one's internal enemies is to annihilate self, a,nd to be
absorbed in the eternity of God, as the light of the stars is lost in the
light of the noonday sun. Everything but God is at once preyed on
by others, and itself preys on others, like the fowl which, when
catching a worm, was itself caught by a cat. Men are so intent on
their own low objects of pursuit that they see not their foes who
are trying to make them their prey. Thus it is said, "Before them
have we set a barrier, and behind them a barrier, so that they shall
not see." 8 Persons who lust after the vile pleasures of this world,
and desire long life, not to serve God, but to satisfy their own carnal
lusts, resemble the crow slain by Abraham, because he only lived
for the sake of carrion; or Iblis, who prayed to be respited till the
day of judgment, not for the purpose of reforming himself but only
to do mischief to mankind. 9
Prayers to God to change our base inclinations and give us higher
aspirations.

O Thou that changest earth into gold,
And out of other earth madest the father of mankind,
Thy business is changing things and bestowing favors,
My business is mistakes and forgetfulness and error.
Change my mistakes and forgetfulness to knowledge;
I am altogether vile, make me temperate and meek.
O Thou that convertest salt earth into bread,
And bread again into the life of men;
Thou who madest the erring soul a guide to men,
And him that erred from the way a prophet; 10
Thou makest some earth-born men as heaven,
And muitipliest heaven-born saints on earth!
But whoso seeks his water of life in worldly joys,
To him comes death quicker than to the rest.
The eyes of the heart which behold the heavens
See that the Almighty Alchemist is ever working here.
Mankind are ever being changed, and God's elixir
Joins the body's garment without aid of needle.
On the day that you entered upon existence,
You were first fire, or earth, or air.
If you had continued in that, your original state,
How could you have arrived at this dignity of humanity?
But through change your first existence remained not
In lien thereof God gave you a better existence
In like manner He will give you thousands of existences,
One after another, the succeeding ones better than the former.
Regard your original state, not the mean states,
For these mean states remove you from your origin.
As these mean states increase, union recedes;
As they decrease, the unction of union increases.
From knowing means and causes holy bewilderment fails;
Yea, the bewilderment that leads you to God's presence.
You have obtained these existences after annihilations;
Wherefore, then, do you shrink from annihilation?
What harm have these annihilations done you
That you cling so to present existence, O simpleton?

Since the latter of your states were better than the former,
Seek annihilation and adore change of state.
You have already seen hundreds of resurrections
Occur every moment from your origin till now;
One from the inorganic state to the vegetive state,
From the vegetive state to the animal state of trial;
Thence again to rationality and good discernment;
Again you will rise from this world of sense and form.
Ah! O crow, give up this life and live anew!
In view of God's changes cast away your life!
Choose the new, give up the old,
For each single present year is better than three past.
This is followed by a commentary on the saying of the Prophet,
"Pity the pious man who falls into sin, and the rich man who falls
into poverty, and the wise man who falls into the company of
fools." This is illustrated by an anecdote of a young deer who was
placed in the asses stable, and jeered at and maltreated by them.
This suggests.
*NOTES:
1. A Hadis.
2. Cp. Bp. Butler, "On a state of probation as implying trial and
danger" (Analogy, Chap. iv. Pt. 1).
3. Probably referring to Origin.
4. Koran ii. 264.
5. Koran iii. 200.
6. Koran vi. 142: "Eat of their fruit, but be not prodigal, and exceed
not."
7. Or, "If there be no supporter, there can be nothing supported."
8. Koran xxxvi. 8.
9. Koran vii. 13.
10. Koran xciii. 7.

STORY IV.

Muhammad Khwarazm Shah and the Rafizis of Sabzawar.
Muhammad Shah was the last prince but one of the Khwarazm
dynasty of Balkh, to which family both the poet's mother and
grandmother belonged. He was the reigning prince in AD. 1209, the
year in which the poet's father fled from Balkh, and was defeated
by Chingiz Khan a year or two later. In one of his campaigns
Muhammad Shah captured the city of Sabzawar, in Khorasan,
which city as inhabited by Rafizis or rank Shi'as, naturally most
obnoxious to a Sunni prince claiming descent from the first Khahif
Abu Bakr. After the city was taken the inhabitants came out, and
proceeded with all humility to beg their lives, offering to pay any
amount of ransom and tribute that he might impose upon them.
But the prince replied that he would spare their lives only on one
condition, viz., that they produced from Sabzawar a man bearing
the name Abu Bakr. They represented to him that it would be
impossible to find in the whole city a single man bearing a name so
hateful to the Shi'as; but the prince was inexorable, and refused to
alter the conditions. So they went and searched all the
neighbourhood, and at last found a traveler lying at the roadside at
the point of death, who bore the name of Abu Bakr. As he was
unable to walk, they placed him on a bier and carried him into the
king's presence. The king reproached them for their contempt and
neglect of this pious Sunni, the only true heart amongst them, and
reminded them of the saying of the Prophet, "God regards not your
outward show and your wealth, but your hearts and your deeds." In
this parable, says the poet, Sabzawar is the world, the poor Sunni
the man of God, despised and rejected of men, and the king is God
Almighty, who seeks a true heart amongst evil men.
Satan's snares for mankind.
Thus spake cursed Iblis to the Almighty,

13

"I want a mighty trap to catch human game withal."
God gave him gold and silver and troops of horses
Saying, "You can catch my creatures with these."
Iblis said, "Bravo!" but at the same time hung his lip,
And frowned sourly like a bitter orange.
Then God offered gold and jewels from precious mines
To that laggard in the faith,
Saying, "Take these other traps, O cursed one."
But Iblis said, "Give me more, O blessed Defender."
God gave him succulent and sweet and costly wines,
And also store of silken garments.
But Iblis said, " O Lord, I want more aids than these,
In order to bind men in my twisted rope
So firmly that Thy adorers, who are valiant men
May not, man-like, break my bonds asunder."
When at last God showed him the beauty of women,
Which bereaves men of reason and self-control,
Then Iblis clapped his hands and began to dance,
Saying, "Give me these; I shall quickly prevail with these!"
This is followed by comments on the text, "Of goodliest fabric we
created man, and then brought him down to the lowest of the low,
saving those who believe and do the things that are right;" 1 and on
the verses,
"If thou goest the road, they will show thee the road;
If thou becomest naught, they will turn thee to being."
*NOTES:
1. Koran xcv. 4.

## STORY V.

### The Man who claimed to be a Prophet.

A man cried out to the people, "I am a prophet; yea, the most excellent of the prophets." The people seized him by the collar, saying, "How are you any more a prophet than we are?" He replied, "Ye came to earth from the spirit-world as sleeping children, seeing nothing of the way; but I came hither with my eyes open, and marked all the stages of the way like a guide." On this they led him before the king, and begged the king to punish him. The king, seeing that he was very infirm, took pity on him, and led him apart and asked him where his home was. The man replied, "O king, my home is in the house of peace (heaven), and I am come thence into this house of reproach." The king then asked him what he had been eating to make him rave as he did, and he said if he lived on mere earthly bread he should not have claimed to be a prophet. His preaching was entirely thrown away on worldly men, who only desire to hear news of gold or women, 1 and are annoyed with all who speak to them of the eternal life to come. They cleave to the present life so fast that they hate those who tell them of another. They say, "Ye are telling us old fables and raving idly;" and when they see pious men prospering they envy them, and, like Satan, become more opposed to them. God said, "What thinkest thou of him who holdeth back a servant of God when he prayeth? " 2

The king then said to him, "What is this inspiration of yours, and what profit do you derive from it?" The man answered, "What profit is there that I do not derive from it? I grant I am not rich in worldly wealth, yet the inspiration God teaches me is surely as precious as that which He taught the bees. 3 God taught them to make wax and honey, and He teaches me nobler things than these. Whoso has his face reddened with celestial wine is a prophet of like disposition with Muhammad, and whoso is unaffected by that spiritual drink is to be accounted an enemy to God and man."

The Prophet's prayer for the envious people.

O Thou that givest aliment and power and stability,
Set free the people from their instability.
To the soul that is bent double by envy
Give uprightness in the path of duty,
Give them self-control, "weigh down their scales," 4
Release them from the arts of deceivers.
Redeem them from envying, O gracious One,
That through envy they be not stoned like Iblis. 5
Even in their fleeting prosperity, see how the people
Burn up wealth and men through envy!
See the kings who lead forth their armies
To slay their own people from envy!
Lovers of sweethearts have conceived jealousy,
And attempted one another's lives,
Read " Wais and Ramin" and "Khosrau and Shirin"
To see what these fools have done to one another.
Lovers and beloved have both perished;
And not themselves only, but their love as well.
'Tis God alone who agitates these nonentities
Making one nonentity fall in love with another.
In the heart that is no heart envy comes to a head,
Thus Being troubles nonentity.

This is followed by an anecdote of a lover who recounted to his
mistress all the services he had done, and all the toils he had
undergone for her sake, and inquired if there was anything else he
could do to testify the sincerity of his love. His mistress replied, "All
these things you have done are but the branches of love; you have
not yet attained to the root, which is to give up life itself for the
sake of your beloved." The lover accordingly gave up his life, and
enjoyed eternal fruition of his love, according to the text, "O thou
soul which art at rest, return to thy Lord, pleased, and pleasing
Him." 6

This is followed by a statement of the doctrine of the jurist Abu
hanifa, to whose school the poet belonged, that weeping, even
aloud, during prayer does not render the prayers void, provided
that the weeping be caused by thoughts of the world to come, and

not by thoughts of this present world. 7 And, apparently in allusion to the name Abu Hanifa, the poet recalls the text, "They followed the faith of Abraham, the orthodox" (Hanifun). 8

*NOTES:

1. Koran iii. 22.
2. Koran xcvi. 9.
3. Koran xvi. 70.
4. Koran ci. 5.
5. Koran xv. 17. The sin of Iblis was his envy of Adam.
6. Koran lxxxix. 27
7. Mishkat ul Masabih, i. p. 209, note.
8. Koran iv. 124.

STORY VI.

The Disciple who blindly imitated his Shaikh.
An ignorant youth entered an assembly of pious persons who were being addressed by a holy Shaikh. He saw the Shaikh weeping copiously, and in mere blind and senseless imitation he copied the Shaikh's behavior, and wept as copiously himself, though he understood not a word of the discourse. In fact, he behaved just like a deaf man who sees those around him laughing, and laughs himself out of compliment to them, though he knows not the subject of their merriment, and is obliged to have it explained to him before he can laugh again with real perception of the joke. After he had wept in this ignorant way for some time he made due obeisance to the Shaikh, and took his departure. But one of the Shaikh's true disciples, being jealous for the honor of his master, followed him, and thus addressed him, "I adjure you by Allah that you go not and say, 'I saw the Shaikh weeping, and I too wept like him.' Your ignorant and mere imitative weeping is totally unlike the weeping of that holy saint. Such weeping as his is only possible to one who has, like him, waged the spiritual war for thirty years. His weeping is not caused by worldly grieves, but by the deep concerns of the spirit. You cannot perceive by reason or sense the spiritual mysteries that are open and plain to his enlightened vision, any more than the darkness can behold the light. His breathings are as those of 'Isa, and not like mere human sighs raised by worldly sorrows. His tears and his smiles and his speeches are not his own, but proceed from Allah. Fools like you are ignorant of the motive and design of saints' actions, and therefore only harm themselves if they try to imitate them, without understanding their meaning." To illustrate this a curious story is told of a foolish lady who copied a trick of her clever slave-girl, without understanding the modus operandi, and by so doing caused her own death. In like manner

18

parrots are taught to speak without understanding the words. The method is to place a mirror between the parrot and the trainer. The trainer, hidden by the mirror, utters the words, and the parrot, seeing his own reflection in the mirror, fancies another parrot is speaking, and imitates all that is said by the trainer behind the mirror. So God uses prophets and saints as mirrors whereby to instruct men, being Himself all the time hidden behind these mirrors, viz., the bodies of these saints and prophets; and men, when they hear the words proceeding from these mirrors, are utterly ignorant that they are really being spoken by "Universal Reason" or the "Word of God" behind the mirrors of the saints. The worthlessness of mere blind imitation (taqlid) of religious exercises.

When a friend tells a joke to his friend,
The deaf man who listens laughs twice over;
The first time from imitation and foolishness,
Because he sees all the party laughing;
Yet, though he laughs like the others,
He is then ignorant of the subject of their laughter;
Then he inquires what the laughter was about,
And, on hearing it, proceeds to laugh a second time.
Wherefore the blind imitator is like a deaf man,
In regard to the joy he feigns to feel.
The light is the Shaikh's, the fountain the Shaikh's,
And the outpouring of joy is also the Shaikh's, not his.
'Tis like water in a vessel, or light through a glass;
If they think they come from themselves, they are wrong.
When the vessel leaves the fountain, it sees its error;
It sees the water in it comes from the fountain.
The glass also learns, when the moon sets,
That its light proceeded from the shining of the moon.
When his eyes are opened by the command, "Arise!" 1
Then that disciple smiles a second time, like the dawn.
He laughs also at his own previous laughter,
Which overtook him out of mere blind imitation.
When he returns from his long and distant wanderings

He says, "Lo! this was the truth, this the secret!
With what blindness and misconception did I pretend.
To experience joy in that distant valley?
What a delusion I was under! what a mistake!
My feeble wit conjured up vain imaginations."
How can an infant on the road know the thoughts of men?
How far its fancies are removed from true knowledge!
The thoughts of infants run on the nurse and milk,
Or on raisins or nuts, or on crying and wailing.
The blind imitator is like a feeble infant,
Even though he possesses fine arguments and proofs.
His preoccupation with obscure arguments and proofs
Drags him away from insight into truth.
His stock of lore, which is the salve of his eyes,
Bears him off and plunges him in difficult questions.
Ah! man of imitation, come out of Bokhara! 2
And humble yourself in order to be exalted.
Then you will, behold another Bokhara within you,
Whereof the heroes ignore these questions of law.
Though a footman may be swift of foot on land,
Yet on the sea he is as one with ruptured tendons.
That footman is only "carried by land," 3
But he who is "carried by sea" is the truly learned one.
The King of kings showers special favors upon him;
Know this, O man pledged to vain illusions!
The mere legal theologian is impotent to behold the light of the
Spirit.
When the day dawns from heaven night flees away;
What, then, can its darkness know of the nature of light?
The gnat scuds away before the blast of the winds;
What, then, knows the gnat of the savor of the winds?
When the Eternal appears the transitory is annulled;
What, then, knows he transitory of the Eternal?
When He sets foot on the transitory He bewilders it;
When it is become naught He sheds his light upon it, 4
If you wish, you can adduce hundreds of precedents,

But I take no heed of them, O man poor in spirit!
The letters Lam, Mim, and Ha, Mim prefixed to some Suras
Resemble the staff of Moses, when fully understood. 5
Ordinary letters resemble these 'to outward view,
But are far beneath them in signification.
If an ordinary man 'take a staff and try it,
Will it prove like the staff of Moses in the test?
This breath of 'Isa is not like every ordinary breath,
Which proceeds from mere human joy or sorrow.
These Alif, Mim, Ha and Mim, O father,
Proceed from the Lord of mankind.
If you have sense, regard not in the same way as these
Every ordinary Alif and Lam which resembles these;
Although these sacred letters consist of common ones,
And resemble common ones in their composition.
Muhammad himself was formed of flesh and skin,
Although no man is of the same genus as he.
He had flesh and skin and bones,
Although no man resembles him in composition;
Because in his composition were contained divine powers,
Whereby all human flesh was confounded.
In like manner the composition of the letters Ha, Mim
Is far exalted above ordinary compounds of letters;
Because from these mysterious compositions comes life,
Even as utter confusion follows the last trump.
That staff becomes a serpent and divides the Nile,
Like the staff of Ha, Mim, by the grace of God.
Its outward form resembles the outward forms of others,
Yet the disk of a cake differs much from the moon's disk.
The saint's weeping and laughter and speech
Are not his own, but proceed from God.
Whereas fools look only to outward appearances,
These mysteries are totally hidden from them;
Of necessity the real meaning is veiled from them,
For the mystery is lost in the intervening medium.
Then follows an anecdote of a man who heard whelps barking in

their mother's womb. A voice came from heaven and explained that these whelps were like the men who have not emerged into the light of truth, but are still veiled in spiritual darkness, and, though they make pretensions to spiritual sight, their discourses are useless, both to procure spiritual food for themselves, and to warn their hearers of spiritual dangers.

Next comes an anecdote of a pious man of Zarwan, who made a point of giving to the poor four times the legal amount of alms due from his growing crops. Thus, instead of paying one-tenth on each crop, which is the legal amount enjoined by the Prophet, 6 he was wont to pay one-tenth of the green ears of corn, another tenth of the ripe wheat, a third tenth of the threshed grain, and a fourth of the bread made therefrom, and so on with grapes and other produce of hi garden. In recognition of his piety God blessed his garden and made it bear fruit abundantly. But his sons, who were blind to spiritual matters, saw only his lavish expenditure upon the poor, and could not see the divine blessing upon the garden, called down by his liberality, and rebuked him for his extravagance. There is no limit to the divine bounty, because God's ability to bestow bounties, unlike human ability, is unbounded and infinite.

*NOTES:

1. Koran lxxiv. 2. Dawn smiles first as "false dawn," and the second time as "true dawn."

2. Alluding to Bokhari, the author of the "Sahih Bokhari," the first and most esteemed collection of traditions.

3. Koran xvii. 72. The man of "external knowledge" is "carried only by land," but the mystic is led over sea as well.

4. When reason is annihilated, the "Truth" is reflected in the resulting caput mortuum or Not-being, as in a mirror (Gulshan i Raz, l. 125).

5. These letters were supposed to have mysterious meanings. See Rodwell, Koran, p. 17, note.

6. Miskat ul Masabih, i. 417.

STORY VII.


How Adam was created out of a handful of earth brought by an Angel.

When the Almighty determined to create mankind to be proved by good and evil, He deputed the angel Gabriel to bring a handful of earth for the purpose of forming Adam's body. Gabriel accordingly girded his loins and proceeded to the Earth to execute the divine commands. But the Earth, being apprehensive that the man so created would rebel against God and draw down God's curse upon her, remonstrated with Gabriel, and besought him to forbear. She represented that Gabriel would at the last day be pre-eminent over all the eight angels who would then support the throne, 1 and that it therefore was only right that he should prefer mercy to judgment. At last Gabriel granted her prayer, and returned to heaven without taking the handful of earth. Then God deputed Michael on the same errand, and the Earth made similar excuses to him, and he also listened to her crying, and returned to heaven without taking a handful. He excused himself to the Almighty by citing the example of the people to whom the prophet Jonah was sent, who were delivered from the threatened penalty in consequence of their lamentation for their sins; 2 and the text, "If He please, He will deliver you from that which ye shall cry to Him to avert." 3 Then God sent the angel Israfil on the same errand, and he also was diverted from the execution of it by a divine intimation. At last God sent 'Izrail, the angel of death, who, being of sterner disposition than the others, resolutely shut his ears to the Earth's entreaties, and brought back the required handful of earth. The Earth pressed him with the argument that God's command to bear away a handful of her substance against her will did not override the other divine command to take pity on suppliants; but 'Izrail would not listen to her, remarking that, according to the canons of theological

23

interpretation, it was not allowable to have recourse to analogical reasoning to evade a plain and categorical injunction. He added, that in executing this injunction, painful though it might be, he was to be regarded only as a spear in the hand of the Almighty. The moral is, that when any of God's creatures do us a harm, we ought to regard them only as instruments of God, who is the Only Real Agent.

God the Only Real Agent.

Do not, like fools, crave mercy from the spear,
But from the King in whose hand the spear is held.
Wherefore do you cry to spear and sword,
Seeing they are captives in the hand of that Noble One?
He is as Azar, maker of idols; I am only the idol;
Whatever instrument He makes me, that I am.
If He makes of me a cup, a cup am I;
If He makes of me a dagger, a dagger am I.
If He makes me a fountain, I pour forth water;
If He makes me fire, I give forth heat.
If He makes me rain, I produce rich crops;
If He makes me a dart, I pierce bodies.
If He makes me a snake, I dart forth poison;
If He makes me a friend, I serve my friends.
I am as the pen in the fingers of the writer,
I am not in a position to obey or not at will.

On the return of 'Izrail to heaven with the handful of earth, God said he would make him the angel of death. 'Izrail represented that this would make him very hateful to men; but God said 'Izrail would operate by disease and sickness, and men would not look for any cause beyond these diseases, according to the text, "He is nearer to you than ye are; yet ye see Him not." 4 Moreover, death is in reality a boon to the spiritual, and it is only fools who cry, "Would that this world might endure for ever, and that there were no such thing as death!"

Death is gain, for "God will change their evil things into good things." 5

One said, "The world would be a pleasant place

24

If death never set foot within it."
Another answered, "If there were no death,
The complicated world would be worth not a jot.
It would be a crop raised in a desert,
Left neglected and never threshed out.
Thou fanciest that to be death, which is life,
Thou sowest thy seed in salt ground.
Carnal reason deceives us; do thou contradict it,
For that fool takes what is really death to be life.
O God, show us all things in this house of deception,
Show them all as they really are!" 6
It is said in the Hadis that on the last day
The command, "Arise," will come to every single body.
The blast of the last trump will be God's command
To every atom to lift its head from the earth.
The souls, also, of each will return to their bodies,
Even as sense returns to bodies awaking from sleep.
On that morn each soul will recognize its own body,
And return to its own ruin like hidden treasure.
It will recognize its own body and enter it.
The soul of the goldsmith will not enter the tailor;
The soul of the wise will enter the body of the wise,
The soul of the unjust the body of the unjust.
In like manner as the souls will fly into their clay,
So will the books fly into their right hands and left. 7
God will place in their hands their books of greed and liberality,
Of sin and piety, and whatever they have practiced.
When they shall awake from sleep on that morning,
All the evil and good they have done will recur to them.
Every thought which has dwelt in them during life
Will appear as a form visible to all, 8
Like the thought of an architect realized in a house,
Or the perfect plant issuing from the seed in the ground.
From onion and saffron and poppy
The hand of spring will unfold the secret of winter.
This one will be verdant and flourish, saying, "We are the pious;"

That other will hang his head like the violet,
With tears starting from his eyes through deadly fear;
Yea, tens of founts of tears through terrible dread;
With eyes wide opened in deadly apprehension
Lest his book may be placed in his left hand.
Then will the evildoer be sent to the fiery prison,
For thorn can in no wise escape the flame.
When his guardian angels behind and before,
Who before were unseen, shall appear like patrols,
They will hurry him off, pricking him with their spears,
And saying, "O dog, begone to thy kennel!"
Then the prisoner will cry, "O Lord, I am a hundred,
Yea, a hundred times as wicked as Thou sayest.
But in mercy Thou veilest my sins,
Otherwise my vileness were known to Thy all-seeing eye.
But, independently of my own works and warfare,
Independently of my faith or unfaith, good or evil,
Independently of my poor devotion to Thee,
And of my thoughts and the thoughts of hundreds like me,
I fix my hopes on Thy mercy alone.
Whether Thou adjudge me upright or rebellious,
I sue for free pardon from Thy unbought justice.
O Lord, who art gracious without thought of consequence,
I set my face towards that free grace of Thine;
I have no regard to my own acts.
I set my face towards this hope,
Seeing that Thou gayest me my being first of all;
Thou gayest me the garment of being unasked,
Wherefore I firmly trust in Thy free grace.
When he thus enumerates his sins and faults,
God at last will grant him pardon as a free gift,
Saying, "O angels, bring him back to me,
Since the eyes of his heart were set on hope,
Without care for consequences I set him free,
And draw the pen through the record of his sins!"
*NOTES:

1. Koran lxix. 17.
2. Koran x. 98.
3. Koran vi 41.
4. Koran lvi. 84.
5. Koran xxv. 70. The "final restitution" of all by free grace.
6. Cp. the Hadis: "Inspiration is a light that shines in the heart, and shows the nature of all things as they really are."
7. See Koran lxix. 18.
8. See the parallel passage in Guishan i Raz, 1. 690.

STORY VIII.

Mahmud and Ayaz. 1

Mahmud, the celebrated king of Ghazni, had a favorite named Ayaz, who was greatly envied by the other courtiers. One day they came to the king and informed him that Ayaz was in the habit of retiring to a secret chamber, and locking himself in, and that they suspected he had there concealed coin stolen from the treasury, or else wine and forbidden drink. The fact was, that Ayaz had placed in that chamber his old shoes and the ragged dress which he used to wear before the king had promoted him to honor, and used to retire there every day and wear them for a time, in order to remind himself of his lowly origin, and to prevent himself from being puffed up with pride. This he did in accordance with the text, "Let man reflect out of what he was created." 2 The intoxication of the present life puffs up many with false pride, even as Iblis, who refused to worship Adam, saying, "Who is Adam, that he should be lord over me?" This he said because he was one of the Jinn, who are all created of fire. 3 Adam, on the other hand, confessed his own vileness, saying, "Thou hast formed me out of clay." The king was well assured of the fidelity of Ayaz; but in order to confute those who suspected him, he ordered them to go by night and break open that chamber and bring away all the treasure and other things hidden in it. It is a characteristic of evildoers to think evil of the saints, because they judge of their conduct by the light of their own evil natures, as the crooked foot makes a crooked footprint, and as the spider sees things distorted through the web he has spun himself The hug's conduct in this did not betoken any diminution of his love for Ayaz, because lover and beloved are always as ono soul, though they may be opposed to outward view. Accordingly the courtiers proceeded to the chamber of Ayaz at night, and broke open the door, and searched the floor and the walls, but found only the old shoes and the ragged dress. They then returned to the king discomfited and shamefaced, even as the wicked who have slandered the saints will be on the day of judgment, according to the text, "On the resurrection day thou shalt see those who have lied of God with their faces black." 4 Then they besought the king to pardon their offence, but he refused, saying that their offence had been committed against Ayaz, and that he would leave it to Ayaz to decide whether they should be punished or pardoned. If Ayaz showed mercy it would be well; and if he punished it would be well also, for "the law of retaliation is the security for life." 5 Only he enjoined him to pronounce his sentence without delay, because "Waiting is punishment."

A description of genuine union with God.
A loved one said to her lover to try him,
Early one morning, "O such an one, son of such an one,
I marvel whether you hold me more dear,
Or yourself; tell me truly, O ardent suitor!"
He answered, "I am so entirely absorbed in you,
That I am full of you from head to foot.
Of my own existence nothing but the name remains
In my being is nothing besides you, O Object of desire!
Therefore am I thus lost in you,
Just as vinegar is absorbed in honey;
Or as a stone, which is changed into a pure ruby,
Is filled with the bright light of the sun.
In that stone its own properties abide not
It is filled with the sun's properties altogether;
So that, if afterwards it holds itself dear
'Tis the same as holding the sun dear, O beloved!
And if it hold the sun dear in its heart,
'Tis clearly the same as holding itself dear.
Whether that pure ruby hold itself dear,
Or hold the sun dear,
There is no difference between the two preterences;
On either hand is naught but the light of dawn.
But till that stone becomes a ruby it hates itself

For till it becomes one 'I,' it is two separate 'I's,'
For 'tis then darkened and purblind,
And darkness is the essential enemy of light.
If it then hold itself dear, it is an infidel;
Because that self is an opponent of the mighty Sun.
Wherefore 'tis unlawful for the stone then to say 'I,
Because it is entirely in darkness and nothingness."
Pharaoh said, "I am the Truth," and was laid low.
Mansur Hallaj said, "I am the Truth," and escaped free.' 6
Pharaoh's "I" was followed by the curse of God;
Mansur's "I" was followed by the mercy of God, O beloved!
Because Pharaoh was a stone, Mansur a ruby;
Pharaoh an enemy of light, Mansur a friend.
O prattler, Mansur's "I am He" was a deep mystic saying,
Expressing union with the light, not mere incarnation. 7
*NOTES:
1. All the latter part of this story is a parable of the last judgement.
2. Koran lxxxvi. 5.
3. Koran xviii. 48, and lv. 14.
4. Koran xxxix. 61.
5. Koran ii. 17.
6. See Guishan i Raz, Answer vii. p. 45. Mansur Hallaj (woolcarder),
the celebrated Sufi who was put to death at Baghdad in 309 (A.H.)
7. See Guishan i Raz, i. 454, and note. The doctrine of the descent of
the Deity into man (Halul), or incarnation, is rejected both by Rumi
and Shabistari in favor of the doctrine of intimate union (Ittihad or
Wahdat).

STORY IX.


The sincere repentance of Nasuh.

Ayaz, in weighing the pros and cons in regard to pardoning the courtiers, remarks that professions of faith and penitence when contradicted by acts are worthless, according to the text, "If ye ask them who hath created the heavens and the earth, they will say 'God;' yet they devise lies." 1 And in illustration of this he tells a story of a faithless husband who retired to a secret chamber ostensibly to say his prayers, but really to carry on an intrigue with a slave-girl, and the falsity of whose pretences was demonstrated by ocular proof of his condition. In like manner, on the day of resurrection man's hands and eyes and feet will bear witness against him of the evil actions done by him, thus confuting his pretences to piety. The test of a sincere repentance is abhorrence of past sins and utter abandonment of all pleasure in them, the old love for sin being superseded by the new love for holiness. Such a repentance was that of Nasuh. Nasuh in his youth disguised himself in female attire and obtained employment as attendant at the women's baths, where he used to carry on shameful intrigues with some of the women who frequented the bath. At last, however, his eyes were opened to the wickedness of his conduct, and be went to a holy man and besought him to pray for him. The holy man, imitating the long-suffering of the "Veiler of sins" did not so much as name his sin, but prayed, saying, "God give thee repentance of the sin thou knowest!" The prayer of that holy man was accepted, because the prayers of such an one are the same as God's own will, according to the tradition, "My servant draws nigh to me by pious works till I love him; and when I love him I am his ear, his eye, his tongue, his foot, his hand; and by me he hears, sees, talks, walks, and feels. "Nasuh then returned to the bath a truly repentant man; but soon afterwards one of the women frequenting the bath lost a

31

valuable jewel, and the king gave order that all persons connected with the bath should be stripped and searched. When the officers came to the bath to execute this order Nasuh was overwhelmed with fear, for he knew that if his sex were discovered he would certainly be put to death. In his fear he called upon God for deliverance, and swooned with fear and became beside himself, so that his natural self was annihilated, and he became a new creature, even as a corpse rising from the grave. When he came to himself he found that the lost jewel had been found, and those who had suspected him came and begged his pardon. Shortly afterwards the king's daughter sent for him to come and wash her head; but, in spite of her imperative commands, he refused to place himself again in the way of temptation, lest he might fall again, and God might "make easy to him the path to destruction." 2

Man's members will bear witness against him on the day of judgement, and confute his claims to piety.
On the resurrection day all secrets will be disclosed;
Yea, every guilty one will be convicted by himself.
Hand and foot will bear testimony openly
Before the Almighty concerning their owner's sins.
Hand will say, "I stole such and such things;"
Lip will say, "I asked for such and such things."
Foot will say, "I went after my own desires;"
Arm will say, "I embraced the harlot."
Eye will say, "I looked after forbidden things;"
Ear will say, "I listened to evil talk."
Thus the man will be shown to be a liar from head to foot,
Since his own members will prove him to be a liar.

*NOTES:
1. Koran xxix. 61.
2. Koran xcii. 10.

STORY X.

The Lion, the Fox, and the Ass.

As an instance of false and insincere repentance, a story is next told, which is also found in the fifth chapter of the Anwar i Suhaili. A lion had been wounded in fight with a male elephant, and was unable to hunt game for himself. In this strait he called a fox who was wont to attend upon him, and to live on the meat that was left from his repasts, just as disciples attending on a saint subsist on the heavenly food dropping from his lips. He called this fox, and bade him go and entice some animal to come near his lair, so that he might kill it and make a meal of it. The fox went and searched the neighborhood, and at last found a lean and hungry ass who was grazing in a stony place where there was little or no grass. The fox, after making due salutations, condoled with the ass on his unfortunate condition; but the ass replied that it was his divinely appointed lot, and that it would be impious to complain of the dispensations of Providence. He also instanced the case of the ass of a water-carrier, which, after having starved and worked hard in its master's service, by chance found admittance to the king's stables, where it was struck by the sleek appearance of the horses. But one day the horses were taken out to battle, and returned in a most miserable plight, some grievously wounded, and others dying. After seeing this sight it determined that its own hard life was preferable, and returned to its master. The fox replied that the ass was wrong in carrying passive resignation to such an extent as to refuse to try to better his condition when the opportunity of doing so presented itself, because God says, "Go in quest of the bounties of God." 1 He added, if the ass would come with him, he would take him to a delightful meadow, where he would never lack plenty of grass all the year round. The ass rejoined that the command to strive for sustenance was only issued on account of the weakness of man's faith. The fox replied that this exalted faith was only vouchsafed to a few great saints, because the Prophet describes contentment as a treasure, and treasure is not found by everyone. The ass rejoined that the fox was perverting the Scripture, as no pious man who trusted in God was ever forsaken. In illustration of this he told an anecdote of a devotee who determined to put the matter to the test, and went out into the desert, trusting only to God to supply his wants, and resolved to seek no aid of man, and not to exert himself in any way to gain food. He lay down on a stone and went to sleep; and God sent a caravan of travelers that way, who found him, and forced him to take food in spite of himself. The fox again pressed the ass to try to better his condition, saying that God had given men hands to use and not to do anything with. The ass answered that he knew of no occupation and exertion better than trust in God, as worldly occupations often lead to ruin, according to the text, "Throw not yourselves with your own hands into ruin." 2 But though the ass repeated all these excellent precepts, yet it was only so much cant on his part, because he was not firmly rooted in. the faith. He had all the time a carnal hankering after the pleasant grazing-ground the fox told him of, and the objections he made were only a parrot-like repetition of precepts heard, but not thoroughly understood and taken to heart. To illustrate the worthless nature of mere imitated religion and profession divorced from practice, a story is told of an infamous fellow who used to carry a dagger to protect as he said, his honor, though his every action showed that he had neither honor to protect nor manliness to protect it. The ass, though like Abraham, he had broken his idols, had not a sufficiently rooted faith to leap, like Abraham, into the fire, and thus prove his faith. [Here the poet apologizes for the trivial illustrations he uses by citing the text, "Verily God is not ashamed to set forth as well the instance of a gnat as of any nobler object" 3.] Finally the ass yielded to the fox's enticement, and accompanied him to the lion's lair. The lion, being famished with hunger, sprang upon him the moment he appeared. Being, however, weak with sickness and fasting, he missed his aim, and the ass escaped with a slight wound. Then the fox blamed the lion for his precipitation, and the lion, after excusing himself as best he could, persuaded the fox to try to allure the ass a second time into his lair. The fox consented to try, observing that experience would probably have been thrown away on an ass, and his vows of repentance forgotten. Those who lapse from repentance, in forgetfulness of their former experience, may be compared to the Jews changed into apes and swine by 'Isa. 4 The fox was received by the ass with many reproaches for having deceived him; but he at last managed to persuade the ass that what he had seen was not a real lion, but only a harmless talisman; and the silly ass allowed himself to be again deluded, and forgot his vows of repentance, and again followed the fox to the lion's lair, where he speedily met his doom.

.

Men who make professions of holiness merely from blind imitation of others are detected and confuted by the opposition between their words and their deeds.
A man asked a camel, saying, "Ho! whence comest thou,
Thou beast of auspicious footstep?"
He replied, " From the hot bath of thy street."
The man said, " That is proved false by thy dirty legs!"
So, when stubborn Pharaoh saw Moses' staff a serpent,
And begged for a delay (to fetch magicians) 5 and relented,
Wise men said, "He ought to have become harsher,
If He really be, as He says, the Lord Supreme. 6
What could miracles such as these of serpents,
Or even dragons, matter to the majesty of His divinity?
If He be really Lord Supreme, seated on His throne,
What need has He to wheedle a worm like Moses?"
O babbler, while thy soul is drunk with mere date wine,
Thy spirit hath not tasted the genuine grapes.
For the token of thy having seen that divine light
Is this, to withdraw thyself from the house of pride.
When a fowl flies to the salt water,
It has never beheld the blessing of sweet water;
But its faith is mere imitation of other fowl,

And its soul has never seen the face of real faith.
Wherefore the blind imitator encounters great perils,
Perils of the road, of robbers, of cursed Satans.
But when he has seen the light of God, he is safe
From the agitation of doubt, and is firm in the faith.
Till the foam has landed on the shore and dry land,
Which is its home, it is ever tossed to and fro.
'Tis at home on the land, but a stranger on the water.
While it remains a stranger, it must be tossed about.
When its eyes are opened, and it sees the vision of land,
Satan has no longer any domination over it.
Although the ass repeated verities to the fox,
He spoke them idly and in the way of cant.
He praised the water, but was not eager to drink;
He rent his garments and his hair, but was no real lover.
The excuse of a hypocrite is rejected, not approved,
Because it comes only from the lips, not from the heart.
He has the scent of the apple, but not a piece of it,
And the scent only for the purpose of misleading others.
Thus a woman's onset in the midst of a battle array,
She keeps in line, and forms part of the battle array,
Yet, though she looks a very lion as she stands in line,
Her hand begins to tremble as soon as she takes a sword.
Woe to him whose reason is like a woman
While his lust is like a resolute man!
Of a certainty his reason will be worsted in the fight,
And his imitation of a man will only lead him to ruin.
Happy is he whose reason is masculine,
And his ugly lust feminine and under subjection!
Though the mere imitator quotes a hundred proofs,
They are all based on opinion, not on conviction.
He is only scented with musk, he is not himself musk;
He smells of musk, but is really naught but dung.
For his dung to become musk, O disciple,
He must graze year after year in the divine pasture.
For he who, like the musk-deer, feeds on saffron of Khoten

Must not eat grass and oats like asses.
That man of cant has at his tongue's end
A hundred proofs and precepts, but there is no life in him.
When the preacher has himself no light or life,
How can his words yield leaves and fruit?
He impudently preaches to others to walk aright,
While himself He is unsteady as a reed shaken by wind.
Thus, though his preaching is very eloquent,
It hides within it unsteadiness in the faith.
In order to gain true wisdom man must shake off worldly illusions.
The fox said, "In my pure wine there are no dregs;
These vain suspicions are not becoming.
All this is only baseless suspicion, O simple one,
Else you would know I am not plotting against you.
You repudiate me on account of your own bad fancies;
Why do you thus suspect your true friends?
Think well of the 'Brothers of purity,' 7
Even though they show harshness toward you;
For when evil suspicion takes hold of you,
It severs you from hundreds of friends.
If a tender friend treats you roughly to try you,
'Tis contrary to reason to distrust him.
Though I bear a bad name, my nature is not malevolent;
What you saw was not dangerous, it was only a talisman.
But even if there were danger in that object of suspicion,
Friends always pardon an offence."
This world of illusions, fancies, desires, and fears,
Is a mighty obstacle in the traveler's path.
Thus, when these forms of delusive imaginations
Misled Abraham, who was a very mountain of wisdom,
He said of the star, " This is my Lord," 8
Having fallen into the midst of the world of illusion.
He thus interpreted the meaning of sun and stars,
Yea, he, that great man who threaded jewels of interpretation,
Seeing then that this world of eye-fascinating illusion
Seduced from the right path such a mountain as Abraham,

So that he said of the star, "This is my Lord,"
What will not its illusions effect on a stupid ass?
Human reason is drowned, like the high mountains,
in the flood of illusion and vain imaginations.
The very mountains are overwhelmed by this flood,
Where is safety to be found save in Noah's ark?
By illusions that plunder the road of faith
The faithful have been split into seventy-two sects.
But the man of conviction escapes illusion;
He does not mistake his eyelash for the new moon.
He who is divorced from 'Omar's light
Is deceived by his own crooked eyelash. 9
Thousands of ships, in all their majesty and pomp,
Have gone to pieces in this sea of illusion.

Then follows an anecdote of Shaikh Muhammad of Ghazni, who
was named "Sar i Razi," because he used to take only a vine-leaf to
break his fast. He dwelt a long time in the desert, and was there
miraculously preserved from death, and directed by divine
intimation to proceed to Ghazni, and beg money of the rich and
distribute it to the poor. After he had done this some time a second
intimation came to him to beg no longer, as the money for his
charities would be supplied to him miraculously. He at last attained
to such a degree of spiritual insight that he knew the wants of those
who came to him for aid before they uttered them. He said the
reason of this preternatural discernment was, that he had purified
his heart of all but the love of God, and thus, whenever thoughts of
anything besides God occurred to his mind, he knew they did not
appertain to him, but must have been in some way suggested to
him by the person asking aid of him.

Then follow some reflections on the power of fasting and
abstinence to subdue the carnal lusts which lead man to
destruction; and two short anecdotes to illustrate the thesis that
God never fails to provide sustenance for those who take no
thought for the morrow, but place absolute trust in Him.

The fate of the ass then suggests to the poet another train of
reflections. After the lion had slain the ass, he went to the river to

quench his thirst, telling the fox to watch the dead body till he returned; but the moment the lion's back was turned the fox ate up the heart and liver, which are the daintiest parts. When the lion returned and inquired for them, the fox assured him that the ass had possessed neither a heart nor a liver, for if he had he would never have shown himself so stupid. Men without understanding are not really men at all, but only simulacra or forms of men. For lack of understanding many will cry in the world to come, "Had we but hearkened or understood, we had not been among the dwellers in the flame" 10 Then follows a story of a monk (Diogenes) who took a lantern and searched all through a bazaar crowded with men to find, as he said, a man.

The monk's search for a man.

The monk said, "I am searching everywhere for a man
Who lives by the life of the breath of God."
The other said, "Here are men; the bazaar is full;
These are surely men, O enlightened sage!"
The monk said, "I seek a man who walks straight
As well in the road of anger as in that of lust.
Where is one who shows himself a man in anger and lust?
In search of such a one I run from street to street.
If there be one who is a true man in these two states,
I will yield up my life for him this day!"
The other, who was a fatalist, said, "What you seek is rare.
But you are ignorant of the force of the divine decree;
You see the branches, but ignore the root.
We men are but branches, God's eternal decree the root.
That decree turns from its course the revolving sky,
And makes foolish hundreds of planets like Mercury.
It reduces to helplessness the world of devices;
It turns steel and stone to water.
O you who attribute stability to these steps on the road,
You are one of the raw ones; yea, raw, raw!
When you have seen the millstone turning round,
Then, prithee, go and see the stream that turns it.
When you have seen the dust rising up into the air,

Go and mark the air in the midst of the dust.
You see the kettles of thought boiling over,
Look with intelligence at the fire beneath them.
God said to Job, 'Out of my clemency
I have given a grain of patience to every hair of thine.'
Look not, then, so much at your own patience;
After seeing patience, look to the Giver of patience.
How long will you confine your view to the waterwheel?
Lift up your head and view also the water."

*NOTES:

1. Koran lxii. 10.

2. Koran ii. 191.

3. Koran ii. 24.

4. Koran v. 65.

5. Koran xx. 25.

6. Koran xxviii. 38.

7. A society at Basra, who wrote, about 980 AD., an encyc1opedia of philosophy (trans. by Dieterici).

8. Koran vi. 76.

9. Alluding to the first anecdote in Book II.

10. Koran lxxvii. 10.

STORY XI.

The Mosalman who tried to convert a Magian.
A Mosalman pressed a Magian to embrace the true faith. The Magian replied, "If God wills it, no doubt I shall do so." 1 The Mosalman replied, "God certainly wills it, that your soul may be saved from hell; but your own evil lusts and the Devil hold you back." The Magian retorted, using the arguments of the Jabriyan or "Compulsionists," that on earth God is sole sovereign, and that Satan and lust exist and act only in furtherance of God's will. To hold that God is pulling men one way and Satan another is to derogate from God's sovereignty. Man cannot help moving in the direction he is most strongly impelled to go; if he is impelled wrongly he is no more to blame than a building designed for a mosque but degraded into a fire-temple, or a piece of cloth designed for a coat but altered into a pair of trousers. The truth is, that whatever occurs is according to God's will, and Satan himself is only one of His agents. Satan resembles the Turkoman's dog who sits at the door of the tent, and is" vehement against aliens, but full of tenderness to friends." 2 The Mosalman then replied with the arguments of the Qadarians and Mutazilites, to prove the freedom of the will and consequent responsibility of man for his actions. He urged that man's free agency and consequent responsibility are recognized in common parlance, as when we order a man to act in a certain way,- that God expressly assumes man to be a free agent by addressing commands and prohibitions to him, and by specially exempting some, such as the blind, 3 from responsibility for certain acts, that our internal consciousness assures us of our power of choice, just as outward sense assures us of properties in material objects, and that it is just as sophistical to disbelieve the declarations of the interior consciousness, as those of the outward senses as to the reality of the material world. He then told an anecdote of a man caught

41

robbing a garden and defending himself with the fatalist plea of irresponsibility, to whom the owner of the garden replied by administering a very severe beating, and assuring him that this beating was also predestined, and that he therefore could not help administering it. He concluded his argument by repeating that the traditions, "Whatever God wills is," and "The pen is dry, and alters not its writing," are not inconsistent with the existence of freewill in man. They are not intended to reduce good action and evil to the same level, but good actions will always entail good consequences, and bad actions the reverse. A devotee admired the splendid apparel of the slaves of the Chief of Herat, and cried to Heaven, "Ah! learn from this Chief how to treat faithful slaves!" Shortly after the Chief was deposed, and his slaves were put to the torture to make them reveal where the Chief had hidden his treasure, but not one would betray the secret. Then a voice from heaven came to the devotee, saying, "Learn from them how to be a faithful slave, and then look for recompense." The Magian, unconvinced by the arguments of the Mosalman, again plied him with "Compulsionist" arguments, and the discussion was protracted, with the usual result of leaving both the disputants of the same opinion as when they began. The poet remarks that the contest of the "Compulsionists" and the advocates of man's free agency will endure till the day of judgment; for nothing can resolve these difficulties 4 but the true love which is "a gift imparted by God to whom He will." 5

Love puts reason to silence.
Love is a perfect muzzle of evil suggestions;
Without love who ever succeeded in stopping them?
Be a lover, and seek that fair Beauty,
Hunt for that Waterfowl in every stream!
How can you get water from that which cuts it off?
How gain understanding from what destroys understanding?
Apart from principles of reason are other principles
Of light and great price to be gained by love of God.
Besides this reason of yours God has other reasons
Which will procure for you heavenly nourishment.
By your carnal reason you may procure earthly food,

By God-given reason you may mount the heavens.
When, to win enduring love of God, you sacrifice reason,
God gives you "a tenfold recompense;" 6 yea, seven hundred fold.
When those Egyptian women sacrificed their reason, 7
They penetrated the mansion of Joseph's love;
The Cup-bearer of life bore away their reason,
They were filled with wisdom of the world without end.
Joseph's beauty was only an offshoot of God's beauty;
Be lost, then, in God's beauty more than those women.
Love of God cuts short reasoning, O beloved,
For it is a present refuge from perplexities.
Through love bewilderment befalls the power of speech,
It no longer dares to utter what passes;
For if it sets forth an answer, it fears greatly
That its secret treasure may escape its lips.
Therefore it closes lips from saying good or bad,
So that its treasure may not escape it.
In like manner the Prophet's companions tell us
"When the Prophet used to tell us deep sayings,
That chosen one, while scattering pearls of speech,
Would bid us preserve perfect quiet and silence."
So, when the mighty phoenix hovers over your head, 8
Causing your soul to tremble at the motion of its wings,
You venture not to stir from your place,
Lest that bird of good fortune should take wing.
You hold your breath and repress your coughs,
So as not to scare that phoenix into flying away.
And if one say a word to you, whether good or bad,
You place finger on lip, as much as to say, "Be silent."
That phoenix is bewilderment, 9 it makes you silent;
The kettle is silent, though it is boiling all the while.
*NOTES:
1. Note the true believer is here represented as using the
arguments of the Qadarians or Mutazilites for free will, as against
the Jabriyan or fatalist argument put into the mouth of the Magian.
2. Koran xlviii. 29.

3. Koran xxiv. 60.

4. The Prophet said, "Sit not with a disputer about fate, nor converse with him."

5. Koran iii. 66.

6. Koran vi. 161.

7. "And when they saw him they were amazed at him, and cut their hands" (Koran xii. 31).

8. It is supposed to bring good fortune.

9. Bewilderment is the "truly mystical darkness of ignorance" which falls upon the mystic when the light of absolute Being draws near to him, and "blinds him with excess of light." See Gulshan i Raz, p. 33, and notes.

STORY XII.

The Devotee who broke the noble's wine-jar.
A certain noble, who lived under the Christian dispensation when wine was allowed, sent his servant to a monastery to fetch some wine. The servant went and bought the wine, and was returning with it, when he passed the house of a very austere and testy devotee. This devotee called out to him, "What have you got there?" The servant said, "Wine, belonging to such a noble." The devotee said, "What! does a follower of God indulge in wine? Followers of God should have naught to do with pleasure and drinking; for wine is a very Satan, and steals men's wits. Your wits are not too bright already, so you have no need to render them still duller by drink." In illustration of this, he told the story of one Ziayi Dalaq, a very tall man, who had a dwarfish brother. This brother one day received him very ungraciously, only half rising from his seat in answer to his salutation, and Ziayi Dalaq said to him, "You seem to think yourself so tall that it is necessary to clip off somewhat of your height." Finally the devotee broke the wine-jar with a stone, and the servant went and told his master. The noble was very wrathful at the presumption of the devotee in taking upon himself to prohibit wine, as condemned by the law of nature, when it had not been prohibited by the Gospel, and he took a thick stick and went to the devotee's house to chastise him. The devotee heard of his approach and hid himself under some wool, which belonged to the ropemakers of the village, He said to himself, "To tell an angry man of his faults one needs to have a face as hard as a mirror, which reflects his ugliness without fear or favor." Just so the Prince of Tirmid was once playing chess with a courtier, and being checkmated, got into a rage and threw the chessboard at his courtier's head. So before playing the next game the courtier protected his head by wrappings of felt. Then the neighbors of the

devotee, hearing the noise, came out and interceded for him with the noble, telling him that the devotee was half-witted, and could not be held responsible for his actions; and moreover, that as he was a favorite of God, 1 it was useless to attempt to slay him before his time, for the Prophet and other saints had been miraculously preserved in circumstances fatal to ordinary persons. The noble refused to be pacified; but the neighbors redoubled their entreaties, urging that he had so much pleasure in his sovereignty that he could well dispense with the pleasure of wine. The noble strenuously denied this, saying that no other pleasure of sovereignty, or what not, could compensate him for the loss of wine, which made him sway from side to side like the jessamine. The prophets themselves had rejected all other pleasures for that of spiritual intoxication, and he who has once embraced a living mistress will never put up with a dead one. The moral is, that spiritual pleasures, typified by wine, are not to be bartered away for earthly pleasures. The Prophet said, "The world is carrion, and they who seek it are dogs;" and the Koran says, "The present life is no other than a pastime and a sport; but the future mansion is life indeed." 2

Description of a devotee who trusted to the light of nature.

His brain is dried up; and as for his reason,
It is now less than that of a child.
Age and abstinence have added infirmity to infirmity,
And his abstinence has yielded him no rejoicing.
He has endured toils, but gained no reward from his Friend;
He has done the work, but has not been paid.
Either his work has lacked value,
Or the time of recompense is not decreed as yet.
Either his works are as the works of the Jews, 3
Or his reward is held back till the appointed time.
This grief and sorrow are enough for him,
That in this valley of pain he is utterly friendless.
With sad eyes he sits in his corner,
With frowning face and downcast looks.
There is no oculist who cares to open his eyes, 4

Nor has he reason enough to discover the eye-salve.
He strives earnestly with firm resolve and in hope,
His work is done on the chance of being right.
The vision of "The Friend" is far from his course,
For he loses the kernel in his love for the shell.

*NOTES:
1. Half-witted persons are supposed to be divinely protected.
2. Koran xxix. 64.
3. "But as to the infidels, their works are like the mirage in the desert" (Koran xxiv. 39).
4. I.e., he has no director (Murshid i kamil) to instruct him in the right course.

STORY VIII.

(continued).
Mahmud and Ayaz.
The poet now returns to the story of Mahmud and Ayaz, which is
continued at intervals till the end of the book. The king inquired of
Ayaz what made him continually visit his old shoes and garments, as
Majnun used to visit his Laila, or as a Christian regularly visits his
priest to obtain absolution for his sins. Why should he call to these
dead things, like a fond mother calling to her dead infant, were it
not that faith and love made them, as it were, living beings to him?
The eye sees what it brings with it to see; it can see nothing but
what it has gained the faculty of seeing. Thus the face of Laila,
which seemed so lovely to the eyes of Majnun, made clairvoyant by
love, seemed to strangers to have no claims to beauty. The earthly
forms which here surround us are, as it were, vessels fraught with
spiritual wine, only visible to those who have learnt to discern the
deep things of the Spirit.
Love and faith are a mighty spell.
O Ayaz, what is this love of yours for your old shoes,
Which resembles the love of a lover for his mistress?
You have made these old shoes your object of devotion,
Just as Majnun made an idol of his Laila!
You have bound the affection of your soul to them,
And hung them up in your secret chamber.
How long will you say orisons to this old pair of shoes?
And breathe your oft-told secrets into inanimate ears?
Like the Arab lover to the house of his dead mistress,
You address to them long invocations of love.
Of what great Asaf were your shoes the house?
Is your old garment, think you, the coat of Yusuf?
Like a Christian who confesses to a priest
His past year's sins of fornication, fraud, and deceit;

48

In order that the priest may absolve him of those sins;
He thinks the priest's absolution the same as God's!
That priest is unable to condemn or to absolve;
But faith and love are a mighty enchantment!
God's dealings visible to the spiritual.
The wine is from that world, the vessels from this;
The vessels are seen, but the wine is hidden!
Hidden indeed from the sight of the carnal,
But open and manifest to the spiritual!
O God, our eyes are blinded!
O pardon us, our sins are a heavy burden!
Thou art hidden from us, though the heavens are filled
With Thy light, which is brighter than sun and moon!
Thou art hidden, yet revealest our hidden secrets!
Thou art the source that causes our rivers to flow.
Thou art hidden in Thy essence, but seen by Thy bounties.
Thou art like the water, and we like the millstone.
Thou art like the wind, and we like the dust;
The wind is unseen, but the dust is seen by all.
Thou art the spring, and we the sweet green garden;
Spring is not seen, though its gifts are seen.
Thou art as the soul, we as hand and foot;
Soul instructs hand and foot to hold and take.
Thou art as reason, we like the tongue;
'Tis reason that teaches the tongue to speak.
Thou art as joy, and we are laughing;
The laughter is the consequence of the joy.
Our every motion every moment testifies,
For it proves the presence of the Everlasting God.
So the revolution of the millstone, so violent,
Testifies to the existence of a stream of water.
O Thou who art above our conceptions and descriptions,
Dust be on our heads, and upon our similitudes of Thee!
Yet Thy slaves never cease devising images of Thee;
They cry to Thee always, "My life is Thy footstool!"
Like that shepherd who cried," O Lord! 1

Come nigh to thy faithful shepherd,
That he may cleanse thy garment of vermin,
And mend thy shoes, and kiss the hem of thy robe!"
No one equaled that shepherd in love and devotion,
Though his manner of expressing it was most faulty.
His love pitched its tent on the heavens,
He himself was as the dog at the tent-door.
When the sea of love to God boiled up,
It touched his heart, but it touches your ears only.

The thesis that silence may indicate emotions too deep for expression, while eloquent expressions may indicate that the ears only, and not the heart, have been touched, is next illustrated by a ludicrous anecdote of a dwarf who disguised himself as a woman, and presented himself at a sermon addressed to women. This dwarf played a trick on a woman sitting next him, which made her cry out, and the preacher fancied that his sermon had touched her heart; but the dwarf said that if her heart had been touched she would not have betrayed her feelings by publishing them to the whole congregation.

The king then again pressed Ayaz to explain the mystery of his regard for the old shoes and rags, in order to admonish the courtiers, for he said that the beauty of true holiness is such that it attracts even infidels. To illustrate this he told an anecdote of a Mosalman who tried to convert a Gueber in the time of Bayazid. The Gueber said that he admired and envied the faith of Bayazid, though he had no power to imitate it; but as for the faith of the missionary who was trying to convert him, it only inspired him with aversion, because it was plainly insincere and hypocritical. And he told an anecdote of a harsh-voiced Mu'azzin who went into a heathen country and there uttered the call to prayer. It happened that there was a girl in that place who had long been inclined to embrace Islam, much to the grief of her parents; but when she heard this harsh call she was at once cured of her wish to forsake her own religion. Her father was so delighted at this that he ran out and loaded the Mu'azzin with gifts. The Gueber said the missionary had cured him of the wish to embrace Islam, just as the girl was cured by the Mu'azzin's harsh voice. But he said he still retained his reverence for the faith of Bayazid, though he failed to understand how so much spirituality as was seen in Bayazid could be contained in an earthly body. He gave a curious illustration of his meaning. A man brought home a piece of meat weighing over half a man, to provide a meal for a guest; but his wife, who was very greedy, ate it all up secretly. When the man missed his meat he asked his wife for it, and she said the cat had eaten it. The man took the cat and weighed her, and found she weighed only half a man. Then he said to his wife, "If this half-man is all cat, where is the meat? and if it is meat, where is the cat?" The Gueber said this was exactly the difficulty he felt about the spirit and the body of Bayazid. He concluded by saying, in the words of the Hadis, "The true believer is attached to others, and others are attached to him, but the hypocrite inspires affection in no one.

Mahmud and Ayaz. (continued).

Mahmud again presses Ayaz to reveal his secrets, remarking that even if they suggest sad thoughts, they will benefit the hearers. The wise man is as a guest-house, and he admits all the thoughts that occur to him, whether of joy or of sorrow, with the same welcome, knowing that, like Abraham, he may entertain angels unawares. This is illustrated by the story of a woman who drove away a valued guest by a petulant remark, which he was not intended to hear, and afterwards repented her discourtesy so deeply that she put on mourning and turned her house into an inn. Let grief as well as joy lodge in the heart, for grief is sent for our benefit as well as joy. Endure woe patiently, like Joseph and Job, and regard it as a blessing, saying with Solomon, "Stir me up, O Lord, to be thankful for Thy favor which Thou hast showed upon me!" 2 Mahmud then praises Ayaz for being a true man who can control both lust and anger. Those who are carried away by anger or lust, like the girl of whom an anecdote is told, do not deserve the name of men. When anger or lust takes hold of a man reason departs from him. Then comes an anecdote of a cowardly Sufi who boasted of his bravery, but had not courage enough even to slay a captive infidel. Verily, the "greater warfare," viz., that against one's own lusts and passions, demands as much courage as the "lesser warfare" against the infidels. This is illustrated by a story of a saint named Iyazi, who, after having been a great warrior against the infidels, renounced the world and applied himself to wage the "greater warfare" against his own lusts. One day, while sitting in his cell, he heard the noise of the army going out to fight, and his carnal passion urged him to go and join in the fight, but he thus rebuked it:

Iyazi's rebuke to his passion, whish lusted to join in the "lesser warfare".

I said, "O foul and faithless passion,
Whence have you derived this inclination to war?
Tell me truly, O passion, is this your trickery?
Or else is it stubbornness shunning obedience to God?
If you say not truly I will attack you,
And will afflict you more severely with discipline."
Passion then heaved a cry from its breast,
And without mouth vented the following complaints:
"In this cell you slay me every day;
You slay my life like the life of a Gueber.
Not a soul is aware of my condition;
You drag me along without food or sleep.
In the fight with one wound I shall quit the body,
And the people will admire my valor and self-devotion."
I said, "O bad passion, you live as an infidel,
And as an infidel you will die; shame be upon you!
In both worlds you are naught but a hypocrite;
In the two worlds only an unprofitable servant.
I have vowed to God never to quit this cell
While life remains in this body;
Because whatever the body does in this privacy
Is not done to make a fair show before men.
Its movements and its rest in the privacy of this cell
Are not intended for the sight of any besides God.
This is the 'greater warfare,' that the 'lesser;'
Both these warfares have their Rustams and Haidars.
They are not to be fought by one whose reason and sense

52

Flee away as soon as a mouse wags its tail.
Such persons must shun the array of battle,
And keep aloof from it even as women do."
This is followed by an anecdote of another brave warrior who "was
among the faithful, and made good what he had promised to God."
3 Then comes a long story of a prince of Egypt who saw the portrait
of a damsel belonging to the Chief of Mausil, and conceived an
ardent passion for her, and sent an army to take her by force. The
army succeeded in capturing her, and set out on the return march;
but on the way the captain of the army fell in love with the damsel,
and she returned his affection. When they reached Egypt she was
made over to the prince, but at once took a dislike to him, as he was
not nearly so manly as her beloved captain. The prince discovered
her secret, and though he might justly have resented the treachery
of the captain, he refrained, and showed true manliness in the
"greater warfare" by pardoning his fault and uniting him with the
damsel to whom he was so much attached.
Ideas gained from hearing a thing lead to seeing it.
A person put this question to a philosopher,
"O sage, what is true and what is false?"
The sage touched his ear and said, "This is false,
But the eye is true and its report is certain."
The ear is false in relation to the eye,
And most assertions are related to the ear. 4
If a bat turn away its eyes from the sun,
Still it is not veiled from some idea of the sun;
Its very dread of the sun frames an idea of the sun,
And that idea scares it away to the darkness.
That idea of light terrifies it,
And makes it cling to the murky night.
Just so 'tis your idea of your terrible foe
Which makes you cling to your friends and allies.
O Moses, thy revelations shed glory on the mount,
But that frightened one endured not thy realities. 5
Be not too proud, but know that you must first endure
The idea of the Truth, and thence come to the reality.

No one is frightened by the mere idea of fighting,
For "no courage is needed before fighting begins." 6
In the mere idea of fighting a coward can imagine
Himself as attacking and retreating like Rustam.
The pictures of Rustam on the wall of a bath
Are similar to a coward's ideas of fighting.
But when these ideas are tested by actual sight,
What of the coward then? His bravery is gone!
Strive, then, from mere hearing to press on to seeing; 7
What ear has told you falsely eye will tell truly.
Then ear too will acquire the properties of an eye;
Your ears, now worthless as wool, will become gems;
Yea, your whole body will become a mirror,
It will be as an eye or a bright gem in your bosom.
First the hearing of the ear enables you to form ideas,
Then these ideas guide you to the Beloved.
Strive, then, to increase the number of these ideas,
That they may guide you, like Majnun, to the Beloved.
Concerning the unbelievers who say, "There is only this our present
life; we live and we die, and naught but time destroyeth us." 8
To return; that prince played the fool,
And took delight in the society of the damsel.
O prince, suppose your dominion extend from east to west,
Yet, as it endures not, esteem it transitory as lightning
Yea, O sleeping heart, know the kingdom that endures not
Forever and ever is only a mere dream.
I marvel how long you will indulge in vain illusion,
Which has seized you by the throat like a headsman.
Know that even in this world there is a place of refuge; 9
Hearken not to the unbeliever who denies it.
His argument is this: he says again and again,
"If there were aught beyond this life we should see it."
But if the child sees not the state of reason,
Does the man of reason therefore forsake reason?
And if the man of reason sees not the state of love,
Is the blessed moon of love thereby eclipsed?

The beauty of Joseph was not visible to his brethren;
Was it therefore hidden from the eyes of Jacob?
The eyes of Moses regarded his staff as a stick,
But the divine eye saw it to be a deadly serpent.
The eye of the head was at issue with the divine eye,
But the latter prevailed and gave convincing proof.
To the eyes of Moses his hand looked a mere hand,
But to the divine eye it appeared a flashing light.
This subject in its entirety is endless,
But to the unbeliever it is a mere fanciful idea.
The only realities to him are lust and gluttony;
Speak not then to him of the mysteries of the Beloved.
To us believers lust and gluttony are only ideas,
Therefore we behold always the beauty of the Beloved.
To all men whose creed is lust and gluttony,
Applies the text, "To you be your creed, to me mine." 10
In the face of negations like these cut short speech,
"O Ahmad, say little to an old Fire-worshipper!"
"We distribute among them," 11 to some carnal lusts, and to others
angelic qualities.
If the prince lacked the animal manliness of asses,
Yet he possessed the true manliness of the prophets.
He renounced lust and anger and concupiscence,
And showed himself a man of the lineage of the prophets.
Grant that he lacked the virility of asses,
Yet God esteemed him a lord of lords.
Let me be dead, so long as God regards me with favor!
I am better off than the living who are rejected of God;
The former is the kernel of manliness, the latter only the rind;
The former is borne to Paradise, the latter to hell.
The Prophet says, "Paradise is annexed to tribulation,
But hell-fire follows indulgence in lust." 12
O Ayaz, who slayest demons like a male lion,
Manliness of asses is naught, manliness of mind much.
What sort of man dost thou think him who sports as a boy,
But who has no comprehension of these chief matters?

o thou who hast seen the delight of my connnandments,
And risked thy life to perform them faithfully,
Hear a tale of the sweetness of my commandments,
That the meaning of this sweetness may be made plain.
The story which follows is one in which Ayaz is himself the chief
actor, and hence it may perhaps be inferred that this part of the
poem had not received its final revision when the poet died. The
king showed to all his courtiers in turn a valuable jewel, and asked
them its value. Each declared it to be priceless. He thereupon
ordered each of them to break it to pieces, but they refused, one
after the other; on which he praised them highly and gave them
presents. Finally the jewel came into the hands of Ayaz, and he, not
being a mere imitator like the rest, nor being tempted by the
rewards given to the rest, decided that the king's command ought
to be obeyed at all costs, and therefore broke the jewel to pieces.
Blind imitation of current fashions and ruling "public opinion" is the
way of the world, but its worthlessness is at once manifested when
it is put to the test. True faith is a reasonable faith, not one adopted
and held in mechanical and parrot-like fashion. The king then
commanded that those courtiers whose faith had been shown to be
mere "taqlid" or imitation, and not vital and intelligent, should be
put to death; but Ayaz interceded for them, saying, "O Lord, punish
them not if they forget or fall into sin;"13 although their plea that
they sinned through forgetfulness is of no more weight than the
plea of having sinned through drunkenness, seeing that both
forgetfulness and drunkenness are willfully incurred. Those who die
in amity with God have no cause to fear death, "It cannot harm
them, for to their Lord will they return;"14 but those who die at
enmity with God are in a very different position, and have therefore
a very strong claim for mercy. The Egyptian magicians, when
threatened by Pharaoh with death for believing in Moses,
recognized the truth that death in such a cause would unite them
with God, and that extinction of the phenomenal self, on which
Pharaoh prided himself, would bring them to the real Self from
whom they had been estranged by life on earth. Like Habib, the
carpenter of Antioch, who was martyred for taking the part of 'Isa's

two apostles in that city, they said, "O that my people knew how gracious God hath been to me, and that He hath made me one of His honored ones!" 15 A man can only say "I" with truth when he has mortified self and unlearnt to say "I" in the sense in which Pharaoh said it. Fakhru-'d-Din Razi 16 discoursed learnedly on this point, saying much of "incarnation" and "union" as the modes in which the real "I" of the Deity indwells in the human soul; but as he lacked the true mystic unction, his words only serve to darken counsel. 17 But here Ayaz breaks off; saying, "Who am I that I should say to the Almighty, 'Grant pardon to these offenders'?" The Omniscient God needs not to be informed of their case, for He knows all; nor to be reminded of it, for He forgets nothing; nor to be urged to act mercifully, for He created men "for their own benefit, and not to derive benefit from them." Such intercession, therefore, implies ignorance of God, and "such only of His servants as are possessed of knowledge of God truly fear God." 18 God is at once center and circumference of the universe, and the only true wisdom consists in absolute self-surrender to His will, and this surrender of self will bring with it its own exceeding great reward.
*NOTES:
1. Alluding to Story vii. Book II.
2. Koran xxvii. 19.
3. Koran xxxiii. 23.
4. i.e., are based on hearsay.
5. "When God manifested Himself to the mount He turned it to dust, and Moses fell in a swoon" (Koran vii. 139). As the bat cannot endure the sight of the sun, men cannot at once endure the full blaze of the beatific vision.
6. A proverb which is not given by Freytag.
7. Ideas and types lead men on to actual sight when they are strong enough to bear it. Job xlii. 5.
8. Koran xlv. 23.
9. Place of refuge, i.e., heavenly visions; a foretaste of the world to come (Gulshan i Raz, I. 679).
10. Koran cix. 6.
11. Koran xliii. 31.

12. Cp. Freytag, Arabum Proverbia, vol ii. p. 165.

13. Koran ii. 286.

14. Koran xxvi. 50.

15. Koran xxxvi. 25.

16. A great theologian of Khorasan who lived from A.D. 1150 to 1210. De Slane's Ibn Khallikan, ii. 652.

17. See Gulshan i Raz, I. 453, note.

18. Koran xxxv. 25.

**End of the book.**